SCHIRMER'S LIBRARY
OF MUSICAL CLASSICS

Vol. 1870

EDOUARD LALO

Concerto in D Minor

For Violoncello and Piano

Edited by
OTTO DERI

ISBN 978-0-7935-6975-5

G. SCHIRMER, Inc.

DISTRIBUTED BY

HAL•LEONARD®
CORPORATION

7777 W. BLUEMOUND RD. P.O. BOX 13819 MILWAUKEE, WI 53213

Concerto in D minor
for violoncello and piano

I

Edited by
Otto Deri

Edward Lalo (1823-1892)

Violoncello

Piano

4

Allegro maestoso. (♩.: 88)

II.

Intermezzo.

Andantino con moto. (♩.=58.)

Concerto in D minor
for violoncello and piano

VIOLONCELLO

Edited by
Otto Deri

Edward Lalo (1823-1892)

I

Intermezzo.
II.

III.

Introduzione.

III.

Introduzione.

26